Zebras

by Anthony D. Fredericks
photographs by Gerry Ellis

Lerner Publications Company • Minneapolis, Minnesota

For Marissa—May her world be filled with exciting adventures, fascinating discoveries, and wonderful treasures! —ADF

To Carol, whose dedication and passion for African creatures has inspired me and so many others to remember that we share this earth with wildlife, and that in doing so we enrich our own lives. —GE

Thanks to our series consultant, Sharyn Fenwick, elementary science/math specialist. Mrs. Fenwick was the winner of the National Science Teachers Association 1991 Distinguished Teaching Award. She also was the recipient of the Presidential Award for Excellence in Math and Science Teaching, representing the state of Minnesota at the elementary level in 1992.

The photograph on page 40 is reproduced with the permission of Feld Entertainment.

Early Bird Nature Books were conceptualized by Ruth Berman and designed by Steve Foley. Series editor is Joelle Riley.

Lerner Publications Company
A division of Lerner Publishing Group
241 First Avenue North
Minneapolis, MN 55401 U.S.A.

Website address: www.lernerbooks.com

Library of Congress Cataloging-in-Publication Data

Fredericks, Anthony D.
    Zebras / by Anthony D. Fredericks ; photographs by Gerry Ellis.
        p.   cm. — (Early bird nature books)
    Includes index.
    Summary: Describes the physical characteristics, behavior, habitat, uses, and endangered status of this black and white striped animal found on the plains of Africa.
    ISBN 0-8225-3043-0 (lib. bdg. : alk. paper)
    1. Zebras—Juvenile literature. [1. Zebras.] I. Ellis, Gerry, ill.
II. Title. III. Series.
QL737.U62 F74 2001
599.665'7—dc21   99-050553

Manufactured in the United States of America
1 2 3 4 5 6 – JR – 06 05 04 03 02 01

Contents

The striped areas on this map show where zebras live.

Be a Word Detective

Can you find these words as you read about the zebra's life? Be a detective and try to figure out what they mean. You can turn to the glossary on page 46 for help.

colt	graze	mane
endangered	habitat	mares
extinct	herbivores	nursing
filly	herd	predators
foal	hooves	stallion

Chapter 1

The plains zebra is the most common kind of zebra. How do zebras tell each other apart?

A Horse of a Different Color

 Everybody notices a zebra's stripes. Different kinds of zebras have different kinds of stripes. No two zebras have exactly the same pattern of stripes. Zebras can tell each other apart by looking at their stripes. That is the way people use fingerprints.

There are three species, or kinds, of zebras. They are the plains zebra, the mountain zebra, and Grevy's zebra. The best known zebra is the plains zebra. You may have seen plains zebras in zoos and circuses. But all wild zebras live in Africa.

Grevy's zebras (above) have narrow stripes. Mountain zebras (left) have broad stripes.

A zebra looks a lot like a horse. That is because zebras, horses, donkeys, and wild asses are all part of the same group of animals. The scientific name for this group is *Equus* (EHK-wuhs).

Horses (left) *and donkeys* (right) *both look a bit like zebras.*

Like horses, zebras have manes.

Grown zebras weigh 500 to 900 pounds. Zebras are 4 to 5 feet tall at the shoulder. Like horses, zebras have long heads and necks. Zebras have big ears, too. They move their ears to hear sounds that are far away.

Zebras use their tails to swat insects.

A short, straight mane runs along the top of a zebra's neck. Zebras have long tails covered with short hair.

A zebra's eyes are set high on the sides of its head. That way a zebra can see all around without moving its head. Zebras can see far away. Even when a zebra bends over to eat or drink, it can watch for enemies.

These zebras are watching for enemies while drinking water.

Chapter 2

Plains zebras live in families. How big are zebra families?

Zebra Families

 Zebras live in family groups. A male zebra is called a stallion (STAL-yuhn). Female zebras are called mares. A family usually has one stallion, a few mares, and several young zebras. Most zebra families have seven to nine members.

A herd of zebras is made up of many families. A herd may have as many as five hundred members.

This herd of zebras is climbing the bank of a river.

A young zebra is in the center of this herd.

Stripes help zebras find each other in a herd. This helps the herd stay together.

Zebras take good care of each other. A whole herd will slow down so young, old, or sick members can keep up.

A herd of zebras usually sleeps on a field with short grass. That way zebras can see any predators (PREH-duh-turz) that might come. A predator is an animal who hunts and eats other animals.

These zebras could be watching for predators.

This young zebra stays close to its mother at night.

Adult zebras can sleep standing up. But they usually lie down at night. While the herd is sleeping, at least one zebra stays awake and standing. That zebra guards the others.

16

Chapter 3

The shrubs are almost as tall as this zebra. What do zebras eat?

Eating and Drinking

 Zebras are herbivores (HUR-buh-vorz). Herbivores are animals who eat plants. Zebras mainly eat long grass. Most zebras live in grasslands. This is their habitat. A habitat is a place where a certain kind of animal can live.

These Grevy's zebras are eating grass.

Plains zebras live on open plains or grasslands. Mountain zebras mostly live on grassy hills and mountains. In cold weather they move to deep, narrow valleys or caves. Grevy's zebras live in dry areas and open grasslands.

Zebras need habitats that have lots of food and water. When a herd of zebras finds a good habitat, it stays there to graze. When zebras graze, they eat grass and other plants. Usually the herd grazes in a small area. But when the land is dry, there is less food and water. Then zebras graze over a larger area.

Sometimes the land is dry. Then zebras have to look for food and water.

Zebras spend most of their time eating or looking for food. They have good teeth for grazing. Their front teeth clip grass easily. They use their back teeth to grind their food.

This zebra has found a good habitat.

Wildebeests sometimes graze with a herd of zebras.

A herd of zebras often will graze with a herd of wildebeests (WILL-duh-beests) or a group of antelopes. Each kind of animal eats a different type of grass. The zebras eat the tall grasses. The wildebeests eat the medium-sized grasses. The antelopes eat the short grasses. That way there is usually enough food for all.

Two antelopes are grazing with a mountain zebra.

Zebras gather at rivers, lakes, and water holes to drink. Sometimes the rivers dry up. But there is still water under the ground. Zebras dig to find it. They use their front hooves to dig. Hooves are a zebra's feet.

Footprints show the shape of a zebra's hooves (top).
Zebras and wildebeests can warn each other of dangers (bottom).

Chapter 4

One zebra is resting its head on another. How do zebras play with each other?

Playing and Fighting

 Young zebras play, just like human children. They race and chase each other across the plains. Sometimes zebras chase after birds or antelopes.

These running games are important. They help young zebras learn how to escape from their enemies. The games help zebras get to know each other, too. This helps keep all the zebras in a herd together.

Zebras are good runners. Running helps keep them strong and healthy.

Zebras groom each other. When they groom, they lick each other clean. One zebra might nibble another zebra's neck and back.

Zebras touch each other. They rub noses. Sometimes zebras rest their heads on each other.

One zebra is nibbling the neck of another zebra to clean it. Zebras take good care of each other.

One zebra is trying to kick another one.

Zebras rarely fight each other. But sometimes stallions fight. They begin by walking around each other. The stallions bite and push each other. They rear up on their back legs. Sometimes they try to kick each other. Finally one stallion runs away. The fight is over.

A zebra is playing by rolling on the ground.

Playing and fighting keep zebras strong. Strong zebras can protect themselves from their enemies.

Chapter 5

A mother zebra nuzzles her baby. How much does a baby zebra weigh when it is born?

Raising Babies

  A baby zebra is called a foal. A female foal is called a filly. A male foal is called a colt.

A foal weighs about 70 pounds when it is born. That is about as much as a large dog. About 20 minutes after it is born, a foal can stand up. After an hour, it can walk.

This young zebra rests its head on its mother's back.
The mother zebra is resting too.

A mare makes sure her foal stays close to
her. That is because the foal has to learn who
its mother is. Mothers and babies learn to

A Grevy's mother stays close to her foal.

know each other's voices, smells, and stripes.
Mares whinny to call their foals. Whinnying is
like the sound of a horse neighing (NAY-ing).

Babies begin nursing, or drinking their mother's milk, shortly after birth. They nurse during their first year of life. They learn to eat grass a few weeks after birth.

A young zebra drinks its mother's milk.

The foal (right) *can run fast enough to keep up with its herd.*

Foals grow quickly. They must be able to run with the herd. The herd is a safe place for a young zebra.

This colt is leaving his herd. He will join a new herd.

A filly usually stays with her mother's herd. But colts leave the herd when they are about two or three years old. They join a herd made up of only colts. When the colts are about five or six years old, they start their own families.

Chapter 6

Zebras and wildebeests watch for predators together. How does a herd of zebras survive?

Living on the Plains

Life on the African plains is hard. But zebras have learned to survive. In a herd, many zebras watch for danger.

Lions are the main enemies of zebras. But wild dogs and hyenas also attack zebras. All of these animals are predators of zebras. Predators often follow a herd of zebras for many miles. They look for zebras who are sick, hurt, or old.

Wild dogs (above left), *lions* (above right), *and hyenas* (below right) *are enemies of zebras.*

Stripes help one zebra to blend in with the others.

You might think that a zebra would be easy to see on the open plains. But that is not true. A zebra's stripes protect it from predators.

Zebras run to escape danger.

A lion standing far away from a herd of zebras chooses a zebra to attack. But one zebra in the herd hears, sees, or smells the lion. The zebra calls out loudly.

Suddenly the herd of zebras begins to move. Now many sets of zebra stripes are moving. The lion quickly loses sight of the one zebra it wanted to attack.

Sometimes lions do chase zebras. But a zebra can run nearly 50 miles per hour. That is nearly as fast as cars go on highways. Zebras can run that fast for long distances. Lions can't run that fast. Zebras can also swim across a river or lake. It is very hard for a predator to capture a healthy adult zebra.

Zebras are good swimmers. They can cross wide rivers.

Chapter 7

*Some zebras work
in circuses. What
other work did
zebras once do?*

People and Zebras

 Long ago, people used zebras as work
animals. In some countries, zebras were trained
to pull carts that a person could ride in. People
also rode zebras as we ride horses.

In modern times, people have hunted zebras for food and for their skins. Zebra skins are worth a lot of money in some countries.

Too much hunting has made some species of zebras endangered. That means there are few zebras of those species left. Those species may become extinct. When a species of animal is extinct, there are none left.

Some people kill zebras for their beautiful skins.

There are many zebras in some parts of Africa.

One species of zebra, the quagga, is already extinct. A quagga had stripes on just its head and neck. Its body was brown. And it had white legs. Early African settlers hunted quaggas for meat. They killed all the quaggas.

In some parts of Africa there are many zebras. In other areas, zebras are in danger because humans have killed too many of them. The mountain zebra is endangered. There are only a few hundred mountain zebras left.

People can help protect the zebras that are still alive. We can all work together to make sure zebras are around forever.

Mountain zebras are endangered.

On Sharing a Book

As you know, adults greatly influence a child's attitude toward reading. When a child sees you read, or when you share a book with a child, you're sending a message that reading is important. Show the child that reading a book together is important to you. Find a comfortable, quiet place. Turn off the television and limit other distractions like telephone calls.

Be prepared to start slowly. Take turns reading parts of this book. Stop and talk about what you're reading. Talk about the photographs. You may find that much of the shared time is spent discussing just a few pages. This discussion time is valuable for both of you, so don't move through the book too quickly. If the child begins to lose interest, stop reading. Continue sharing the book at another time. When you do pick up the book again, be sure to revisit the parts you have already read. Most importantly, enjoy the book!

Be a Vocabulary Detective

You will find a word list on page 5. Words selected for this list are important to understanding the topic of this book. Encourage the child to be a word detective and search for the words as you read the book together. Talk about what the words mean and how they are used in the sentence. Do any of these words have more than one meaning? You will find these words defined in a glossary on page 46.

What about Questions?

Use questions to make sure the child understands the information in this book. Here are some suggestions:

> What did this paragraph tell us? What does this picture show? What do you think we will learn about next? What do you think it's like being a zebra? How are zebras like horses? How are they different from horses? Can zebras see well? Can they hear well? What do zebras eat? What do you like most about zebras? What is your favorite part of the book? Why?

If the child has questions, don't hesitate to respond with questions of your own, such as: What do *you* think? Why? What is it that you don't know? If the child can't remember certain facts, turn to the index.

Introducing the Index

The index is an important learning tool. It helps readers get information quickly without searching throughout the whole book. Turn to the index on page 47. Choose an entry, such as *stripes,* and ask the child to use the index to find out how stripes help zebras. Repeat this exercise with as many entries as you like. Ask the child to point out the differences between an index and a glossary. (The index helps readers find information quickly while the glossary tells readers what words mean.)

All the World in Metric!

Although our monetary system is in metric units (based on multiples of 10), the United States is one of the few countries in the world that does not use the metric system of measurement. Here are some conversion activities you and the child can do using a calculator:

WHEN YOU KNOW:	MULTIPLY BY:	TO FIND:
miles	1.609	kilometers
feet	0.3048	meters
inches	2.54	centimeters
gallons	3.787	liters
tons	0.907	metric tons
pounds	0.454	kilograms

Activities

Imagine being a zebra. What would a day in a zebra's family be like? Make up a story about it. Draw pictures to go with your story.

Visit a zoo or wild animal preserve where zebras can be found. Spend some time watching them. During a five-minute time period, what do they do? How do they behave when they are by themselves? How do they behave in a group?

Make a zebra book. Write down some interesting facts you learned from this book. Write down some facts about the zebras you saw at the zoo. Add some information from other books to your zebra book.

Glossary

colt—a young male zebra

endangered—having only a few of a kind of animal still living

extinct—having no members of a kind of animal still living

filly—a young female zebra

foal—a zebra less than one year old

graze—to eat grass and other plants

habitat—an area where a kind of animal can live and grow

herbivores (HUR-buh-vorz)— animals who eat only plants

herd—a large group of zebras

hooves—a zebra's feet

mane—a strip of bushy hair on top of a zebra's neck

mares—female zebras

nursing—drinking mother's milk

predators (PREH-duh-turz)— animals who hunt other animals for food

stallion (STAL-yuhn)—a male zebra

Index

Pages listed in **bold** type refer to photographs.

About the Author

Anthony D. Fredericks is a former elementary classroom teacher now working as Professor of Education at York College in York, Pennsylvania. He has taken many advanced courses in zoology, environmental studies, anatomy, and oceanography. He has written nearly 300 articles and more than three dozen books, including college textbooks, teacher resource books, and children's books. His children's books focus on animals, environmental concerns, and nature activities for kids of all ages. Several of his books have won special awards and citations. His favorite hobby is writing. Every year he visits many schools as a professional storyteller, science consultant, and visiting author. In his free time he enjoys traveling, snorkeling, hiking, and exploring.

About the Photographer

Gerry Ellis has explored the world as a professional photographer and naturalist for nearly two decades. His images of wildlife and natural landscapes have won him many awards, including several honors in the BBC Wildlife Photographer of the Year competition. Among his many publications are the Lerner Publishing Group titles *Hippos, Cheetahs, Rhinos, African Elephants,* and *Slugs.* Mr. Ellis lives in Portland, Oregon.

The Early Bird Nature Books Series

African Elephants	Manatees	Scorpions
Alligators	Moose	Sea Lions
Ants	Mountain Goats	Sea Turtles
Apple Trees	Mountain Gorillas	Slugs
Bobcats	Ostriches	Swans
Brown Bears	Peacocks	Tarantulas
Cats	Penguins	Tigers
Cougars	Polar Bears	Venus Flytraps
Crayfish	Popcorn Plants	Vultures
Dandelions	Prairie Dogs	Walruses
Dolphins	Rats	Whales
Giant Sequoia Trees	Red-Eyed Tree Frogs	Wild Turkeys
Herons	Saguaro Cactus	Zebras
Jellyfish	Sandhill Cranes	